Copyright © 2012 Tanya Kabes Lauro
Cover and book design by Carrie Medeiros
Edited by Melissa Ball and Geraldine Duncan
Portrait photography by Eric Synder

All rights reserved. No portion of this book may be reproduced or transmitted in any form or by any means, electronic or mechanical—including fax, photocopy, recording, or any information storage and retrieval system—without the written permission of the author, except as granted under the following conditions:

- The purchaser may photocopy pages for personal use.
- A reviewer may quote brief passages in connection with a review written for inclusion in a blog, magazine, or newspaper, with written approval from the author prior to publishing.

The information provided in this book is designed to provide helpful information on the subjects discussed. This book is not meant to be used, nor should it be used, to diagnose or treat any medical condition. For diagnosis or treatment of any medical problem, consult your own physician. The publisher and author are not responsible for any specific health or allergy needs that may require medical supervision and are not liable for any damages or negative consequences from any treatment, action, application, or preparation, to any person reading or following the information in this book.

I would like to give a very special thank you to:

Carrie Medeiros, who was the designing force behind my dream. She is the owner and graphic designer of Graceline Studios, which is a New Hampshire based marketing and design firm.

My editor, Melissa Ball, for making sure the wording in my book was correct before we sent it to print. Melissa spent many hours combing through and perfecting each page on a tight deadline. I am extremely grateful for her exceptional work.

Eric Synder, the mastermind behind my personal photographs.

TANYA KABES LAURO

Meet Tanya

"I never would have thought that at 35 years of age I would feel and look the best I have in my life. Through the years, I have changed many aspects of my life in order to benefit my health in the long run."

A warrior is often seen as a fighter who rises above all obstacles in life, perseveres, and ultimately becomes successful. Tanya Kabes Lauro is a warrior in her own right.

After being initially turned away by the US Navy in 1995 for being "overweight" by their standards, Tanya decided to do a complete lifestyle overhaul and focus on her health and well-being through exercise and clean-eating. She cut her food intake and started experimenting with different ingredients to create healthy recipes that interested and enticed her.

Tanya quickly lost enough weight to be accepted into the Navy's training program and found herself waking up at 4:00 every morning for two months to participate in their intense and sometimes grueling activities. She ended up losing 60lbs by the program's end. Tanya is a proud Navy veteran and says she learned the true meaning of honor, courage, and commitment while she served.

In more recent years, Tanya traded in the Navy uniform for 6" high heels and bikinis, competing and placing in many local fitness and figure competitions. She is just as comfortable throwing around weights in the gym as she is strutting down the runway for competitions.

You will find Tanya in the gym at least five times a week, as she believes achieving optimum health includes physical fitness in addition to healthy-eating. After trying out different gyms in the area, Tanya settled in as a member of CrossFit TUFF, located in Nashua, NH. Becoming a member there has given her the ultimate opportunity, through positive and professional guidance, to transform her body in a safe and healthy way.

At home, Tanya enjoys growing her own organic food to include in many of her recipes. While she has a passion for food and fitness, she also holds a love for children. Tanya is a nanny and often uses her organic ingredients to create healthy meals for the children she cares for each day. In her kitchen, you will typically find Tanya testing out different meals and cooking with her two Yellow Labradors, Lexi and Sadie, curled up next to her feet.

Tanya's hope for Food for the Warrior is to provide a guideline for healthy meals to fit everyone's lifestyle and palate, while keeping it interesting and fun. She believes that with a little leadership and support, everyone can obtain their goals and become warriors in life.

nu-tri-
nu-tri-ti
see nour

table of contents

- **10** — kitchen tips
- **16** — breakfast & shakes
- **28** — snacks & sides
- **46** — primitive plates
- **76** — desserts
- **90** — condiments

My Kitchen Staples

There are a few items that you will always find in my kitchen. You will see in many of my recipes, that I often turn to these products, so I always stock up when I grab a chance!

- Almond & coconut flour *(great for cakes, pies, muffins)*
- Coconut oil, rice bran oil, olive oil *(good for use in everyday cooking, baking, and stir-fries)*
- Fresh vegetables: Asparagus, Brussels sprouts, spinach, carrots, peppers, cucumbers, kale, spaghetti squash, and butternut squash.
- Eggs
- Barley
- Quinoa
- Mrs. Dash® seasoning *(every variety)*
- Almond butter
- Nuts *(every variety, kept in canning jars)*
- Fruits: Bananas, apples, oranges, and grapefruits

Quick Tips

- Buy nuts in bulk and put them into serving-size bags for a quick snack when you're on the go.

- Buy meat in bulk to save on cost. Some meat, such as buffalo, tends to go on sale in the winter months, so buy a lot and freeze it. It will last in the freezer for up to a year if sealed properly.

- Prepare meals for the week in advance. Choose a day for preparation, grocery shop, prepare, and store until ready to cook.

- Slow cookers are great tools for cooking meals while you are away for the day. There is sometimes nothing better than coming home after a long day at work to a meal that is ready to eat!

Kitchen Gadgets I Can't Live Without

Just like my food and spice staples, there are a few kitchen gadgets that I can't imagine my life without. These not only help me create meals I enjoy, but make preparation a lot easier!

- **Skillet:** I cook my meats, eggs, and vegetables in it. It is great for that summer-grill look during the winter months.

- **Food processor:** I love using this to make purees, nut butters, sauces, and homemade sausages.

- **Mixer:** I usually find myself making smoothies with this.

- **Meat mallet:** I use this to tenderize the lean meats that have hard connective tissue.

- **Ziploc® bags:** I put my marinades in them for easy clean up.

Seasonal Eating and Why It's Important

Buying produce while it is considered "in season" provides some benefits. I find that when I eat produce in the proper season, it not only tastes better, but I also pay less. Here is a chart to help you determine seasonal produce and achieve ultimate ripeness while padding your wallet at the same time.

Season	Month	Produce
Spring	March	Greens
Spring	April	Asparagus, Kale
Spring	May	Asparagus, Broccoli, Cauliflower, Green Peas, Kale, Potatoes, Spinach, Strawberries,
Summer	June	Asparagus, Blueberries, Cabbage, Corn (sweet), Cucumbers, Eggplant, Green Peas, Peppers, Potatoes, Raspberries, Snap Beans, Squash, Strawberries, Tomatoes
Summer	July	Beets, Blackberries, Black Eyed Peas, Blueberries, Cabbage, Cantaloupes, Carrots, Cider, Corn (sweet), Cucumbers, Eggplant, Green Peas, Lima Beans, Nectarines, Okra, Peaches, Peppers, Plums, Potatoes, Raspberries, Snap Beans, Squash, Tomatoes, Watermelons
Summer	August	Apples, Beets, Blackberries, Black Eyed Peas, Blueberries, Broccoli, Cabbage, Cantaloupes, Carrots, Cider, Corn (sweet), Cucumbers, Eggplant, Grapes, Lima Beans, Nectarines, Okra, Peaches, Pears, Peppers, Plums, Potatoes, Raspberries, Snap Beans, Squash, Tomatoes, Watermelons
Autumn	Sept.	Apples, Beets, Broccoli, Cabbage, Cantaloupes, Carrots, Cauliflower, Cider, Corn (sweet and Indian), Cucumbers, Eggplant, Gourds, Grapes, Kale, Lima Beans, Peaches, Pears, Plums, Peppers, Potatoes, Pumpkins, Snap Beans, Squash, Sweet Potatoes, Tomatoes, Watermelons
Autumn	Oct.	Apples, Broccoli, Cauliflower, Corn (Indian), Cucumbers, Gourds, Kale, Lima Beans, Pears, Snap Beans, Peppers, Pumpkins, Spinach, Sweet Potatoes, Squash
Autumn	Nov.	Apples, Greens, Pumpkins, Spinach, Sweet Potatoes
Winter	Dec.	Greens, Sweet Potatoes
Winter	Jan.	Greens
Winter	Feb.	Greens

Dry Weight Measurements

		Ounces	Pounds	Metric
1/16 tsp	a dash			
1/8 tsp or less	a pinch or 6 drops			.5 ml
1/4 tsp	15 drops			1 ml
1/2 tsp	30 drops			2 ml
1 tsp	1/3 Tbsp	1/6 oz		5 ml
3 tsp	1 Tbsp	1/2 oz		14 g
1 Tbsp	3 tsp	1/2 oz		14 g
2 Tbsp	1/8 cup	1 oz		28 g
4 Tbsp	1/4 cup	2 oz		56.7 g
5 Tbsp plus 1 tsp	1/3 cup	2.6 oz		75.6 g
8 Tbsp	1/2 cup	4 oz	1/4 lb	113.4 g
10 Tbsp plus 2 tsp	2/3 cup	5.2 oz		158 ml
12 Tbsp	3/4 cup	6 oz	.375 lb	177 ml
16 Tbsp	1 cup	8 oz	1/2 lb	225 ml
32 Tbsp	2 cups	16 oz	1 lb	450 ml
64 Tbsp	4 cups or 1 qt	32 oz	2 lbs	907 ml

Why I Love Coconut Oil

Coconut oil is noted as providing numerous benefits to the overall general care and health of the human body. You will find many of the recipes in this book include coconut oil, as I have personally benefitted from the use of it. Here are just a few reasons why I believe coconut oil is an important addition to your daily lifestyle.

Digestion » Coconut oil is easily digestible and often finds its way into recipes as cooking oil. Coconut oil helps in the absorption of vitamins, minerals, and amino acids. It may aid in prevention of stomach and digestion-related issues countless individuals experience each day.

Weight Loss » Although there have not been any definitive finds in studies done on this topic, I have personally found that coconut oil is beneficial in weight loss. As it is classified as a "functional food," it provides an immense amount of health benefits reaching beyond its nutritional content. It has been noted that it boosts energy and endurance, as well as metabolism, which often promotes healthy weight loss. It is important to note, however, that coconut oil is high in calories, so monitor when including it as part of your calorie-balanced diet.

Skin Care » I have spoken with many individuals who swear by coconut oil as a benefit to skin care. Because of its natural origin, it is found as a safe way to prevent everyday dryness and flaking of skin without any of the harmful effects one might find in processed products. Many believe it holds off the production of wrinkles and sagging of the skin as age progresses. You will find that coconut oil is oftentimes listed in some of the basic ingredients in body care products, as users note positive treatment of some skin infections, including eczema, dermatitis, and psoriasis.

Hair Care » It has been shown that coconut oil is greatly beneficial to the nutrition of your hair. Regular application of coconut oil to the scalp reduces the signs of dandruff and creates a shiny complexion. It is also a great conditioner, even for damaged hair.

There are many additional benefits of coconut oil not listed here. As with anything, research and consult with your doctor about the pros and cons of adding coconut oil into your regular diet and daily care routine.

Coconut Flour

»› To bake with 100% coconut flour ›»

WHEAT IN RECIPE	COCONUT FLOUR	INCREASE EGGS	INCREASE LIQUIDS
1 cup =	⅓ cup +	one egg + per oz/flour	more water/ coconut milk

»› To use coconut flour in small doses ›»

RECIPE CALLS FOR	ADD GRAIN FLOUR	ADD COCONUT FLOUR	INCREASE LIQUIDS
2 cups = grain flour	1 cup +	1 cup +	1 cup

breakfast & shakes

Banana Nut Muffins

Ingredients
½ cup coconut flour
½ tsp sea salt
½ tsp baking soda
6 eggs
¼ cup raw honey
3 bananas
⅓ cup coconut oil
1 tsp vanilla extract
1 cup walnut pieces

Directions
Preheat oven 350°F. In a small bowl, combine coconut flour, salt, and baking soda. In a blender, puree bananas. In a large bowl, mix eggs, honey, bananas, coconut oil, and vanilla until well blended. Mix dry ingredients into the wet, blending with a hand mixer or by hand. Gently fold in walnut pieces. Use a cupcake pan lined with aluminum cupcake inserts and pour batter until inserts are roughly ½ - ¾ full. Bake 12-14 minutes.

Almond Banana Pancakes

Ingredients
2 ripe bananas
1 egg
1 heaping Tbsp almond butter

Directions
Mash bananas and add egg, mixing well. Stir in almond butter until smooth *(you may want to add more almond butter to make the consistency like pancake batter)*. In a hot skillet coated with an oil spray, add one Tbsp of mixture to the pan. Brown on both sides and serve with agave nectar or fresh fruit.

Optional add-ins: nuts, dark chocolate chips

Berry Nella Shake

Ingredients
⅓ cup frozen berries
¼ cup coconut water
1 scoop whey protein *(I use Syntrax® brand Nectar Vanilla Torte)*
½ tsp vanilla
Sprinkle cinnamon or fresh mint

Directions
In a blender, add all ingredients and mix until smooth.

Blueberry Kale Shake

Ingredients
½ cup frozen blueberries
¼ cup coconut water
1 stalk kale, chopped *(stem removed)*
1 scoop whey protein *(I use Syntrax® brand Nectar Vanilla Torte)*

Directions
Add all ingredients to a mixer and blend until smooth. You can add ice if you want it thicker.

Tip: Kale is easiest to blend if you either boil it for 1-2 minutes or put it in the freezer for at least 30 minutes.

Veggie Quiche

Ingredients
7 eggs
1½ cups fresh spinach, chopped
1 cup broccolettes *(roughly chopped broccoli works too)*
1 green onion, thinly sliced
1 small yellow onion, chopped
3 cloves garlic, minced
½ cup coconut milk
¾ tsp baking powder
Salt and freshly ground black pepper to taste

Directions
Preheat oven 350°F. In a large bowl, whisk eggs and coconut milk together until thoroughly combined. Add remaining ingredients. Grease a 9" pie dish with coconut oil. Sprinkle almond meal evenly and tip the dish, making sure it sticks to all sides. Dump out any excess. Bake quiche about 40 minutes, or until cooked through in center.

Egg Cupcakes

Ingredients
1 carton of eggs *(use 12 whites and only 6 yolks)*
¼ cup red bell peppers
½ cup zucchini, diced small
4 slices bacon, cooked and crumbled
2 cups spinach
Black pepper to taste

Directions
Preheat oven 350°F. Whisk eggs and pepper. Add remaining ingredients and stir thoroughly. Add to cupcake tins evenly. Bake 20-25 minutes.

Optional add-ins: Sausage, bacon, ham, onion

Broccoli Frittata

Ingredients
10 eggs
½ cup red onion
1½ cup broccoli, finely chopped
1 cup mushrooms, diced
1 tsp garlic powder
2 Tbsp coconut oil
Salt and pepper to taste

Directions
Warm coconut oil in a pan. Sauté onions until caramelized. Add mushrooms and broccoli and sauté until broccoli is soft, roughly 5 minutes. Spread vegetable mix across bottom of pan. Add eggs, sea salt, pepper, and garlic powder by gently pouring over top of vegetables until eggs are cooked.

Sweet Potato Hash Browns

Ingredients
2 or 3 sweet potatoes
½ cup leeks, finely chopped
2 Tbsp rice bran oil or olive oil
½ tsp parsley
½ tsp garlic
½ tsp chives
½ tsp chili pepper
½ tsp onion powder
½ tsp sesame seeds
1 tsp chipotle pepper sauce

Directions
Peel sweet potatoes. Grate potatoes using a cheese grater. Mix with leeks, salt, pepper, and spices, and toss until everything is combined. Heat olive oil in a pan on medium-high. Add sweet potato/leeks mix and cook gently, stirring periodically. Cook 5 minutes or until desired texture.

Breakfast Pizza

Ingredients
10 eggs
¼ lb sausage *(I use turkey)*
¼ cup red onions
½ cup cherry tomatoes, chopped
¼ cup red peppers
2 tsp coconut oil

Directions
Crack eggs into a small dish and whisk together. In a sauté pan, heat coconut oil. Add sausage and cook. Add onions, red peppers, and cook until soft. Set aside. Spray a pan for eggs, so they don't stick. Use 3 eggs for each person and top with mixture.

snacks & sides

7 Layer Fiesta Dip

Ingredients
2 lbs lean ground turkey, buffalo, or Angus burger

Tomato layer:
4 large tomatoes, cored, seeded, and finely chopped
1 jalapeno, seeded and minced
3 Tbsp cilantro, finely chopped
2 green onions, finely minced
2 Tbsp lime juice *(from about 2 limes)*
1/8 tsp salt

Guacamole layer:
2 green onions, sliced thin, green and white parts separated
1 jalapeno chile, seeded and finely minced
1 small garlic clove, minced
2 Tbsp lime juice *(from about 2 limes)*
3 avocados, pitted, peeled, and chopped
3 Tbsp fresh cilantro, chopped
Salt to taste

Black bean layer:
1 16-oz can black beans, drained but not rinsed
2 garlic cloves, minced
2 Tbsp fresh lime juice *(from about 1 lime)*
3/4 tsp chili powder
1/4 tsp salt

Sour cream layer:
1 1/2 cups fat free sour cream or plain fat free yogurt
1 cup shredded low fat pepper jack cheese
1 cup shredded low fat sharp cheddar cheese

Cheese layer:
1 cup shredded low fat pepper jack cheese

Directions

Tomato layer:
In a medium bowl, combine tomatoes, jalapeno, cilantro, minced green onions, and lime juice. Stir in salt and let stand until tomatoes begin to soften, about 30 minutes. Strain mixture through a fine mesh strainer or colander and discard liquid. Set aside.

Guacamole layer:
In a small bowl, combine white parts of green onions, jalapeno, garlic, and lime juice. Let sit 30 minutes. Add two-thirds of avocado to bowl with jalapeno mixture and mash with a potato masher until smooth. Gently fold remaining avocado into mashed avocado mixture. Gently stir in green parts of green onions and cilantro. Season with salt. Set aside.

Pulse black beans, garlic, remaining lime juice, chili powder, and remaining salt in a food processor until mixture resembles a chunky paste. Sauté meat with a tsp of olive oil and set aside to cool. Transfer meat to an 8x8" glass or similar-sized bowl, spreading into an even layer. Add bean mixture on top. Quickly rinse and wipe out food processor and pulse sour cream, 1 cup pepper jack cheese, and 1 cup sharp cheddar cheese until smooth. Dollop sour cream mixture on top of black bean layer, smoothing to the edges evenly.

Sprinkle evenly with remaining cheese. Spread guacamole over cheese and top with tomato mixture. Sprinkle with additional sliced green onions, if desired, and serve with tortilla chips. The dip can be tightly covered and refrigerated for up to 24 hours.

Sweet Potato Chips

Ingredients
2 sweet potatoes, sliced thin
2 Tbsp coconut oil, melted
½ tsp sea salt

Directions
Preheat oven 400°F. Add potatoes in a bowl and cover with melted coconut oil and salt. Line a cookie sheet with foil and arrange sweet potatoes. Cook 14 minutes on one side, remove from oven, flip, and cook an additional 10 minutes.

Sweet Pea Guacamole

Ingredients
2 medium Haas avocados, seeded and chopped
1 cup sweet peas, thawed
½ cup cherry tomatoes
3 green onions, chopped
1 tsp jalapenos, seeded and chopped
1½ tsp lemon

Directions
In a bowl, smash peas and avocados. Set aside. In a small bowl, mix onions, jalapenos, lemon juice, cherry tomatoes, and add to pea and avocado mixture. Serve chilled.

Cayenne Spiced Nuts

Spice ingredients
2 tsp all natural sugar
1½ tsp sweet paprika
1½ tsp ground cumin
1 tsp cayenne pepper
½ tsp garlic powder
¼ tsp ground allspice

Nut ingredients
2 cups raw cashews
2 cups dried cranberries
1 cup raw pecans
½ cup raw pumpkin seeds
½ cup raw sunflower seeds
3 Tbsp olive oil

Directions
Preheat oven 300°F. Combine all dry ingredients. Add oil. Spread mixture onto 2 baking sheets. Cook 25-30 minutes.

Almond Energy Bars

Ingredients
1½ cup almond flour
¼ tsp baking soda
¼ cup coconut oil, melted
½ cup raw honey
2 tsp vanilla extract
½ cup shredded unsweetened coconut
½ cup pumpkin seeds
½ cup sunflower seeds
½ cup slivered almonds
½ cup mini dark chocolate chips

Directions
Preheat oven 350°F. In a small bowl, combine almond flour, baking soda, and set aside. In a large bowl, combine coconut oil, honey, and vanilla, mixing well. Mix dry ingredients into wet ingredients. Mix in shredded coconut, pumpkin seeds, almonds, sunflower seeds, and mini chips. Grease an 8x8" dish with coconut oil. Press mixture firmly into dish *(you may have to wet your hands first)*. Bake 20-25 minutes. Cool 5 minutes.

This should make 16 bars. You can double the ingredients for more.

Trail Hike Bars

Ingredients
1 cup organic sunflower seed butter
1 cup sweetened coconut flakes
½ cup mini chocolate chips *(I use Enjoy Life® brand)*
½ cup organic brown sugar
½ cup cranberries
½ cup dates, chopped
¼ cup sunflower seeds
¼ cup agave nectar
1 large egg
1 tsp vanilla extract
½ tsp baking soda
¼ tsp salt *(optional)*

Directions
Preheat oven 350°F. Place ingredients in a large mixer. Mix until well blended. Form balls and drop onto a cookie sheet lined with parchment paper. Bake 12-14 minutes. Cool 5 minutes.

Flaky Quinoa Cakes

Ingredients
1 large egg
2 Tbsp almond flour
1½ Tbsp tahini
1½ tsp white wine vinegar
1½ cup whole wheat quinoa, cooked
½ cup sweet potato, finely grated
½ cup frozen spinach, thawed and squeezed
¼ cup sun dried tomatoes, chopped
¼ cup walnuts, finely chopped
2 Tbsp onions, finely chopped
1 Tbsp fresh parsley, chopped
1 tsp garlic, minced

Directions
Preheat oven 350°F. Coat baking sheet with spray. Combine egg, almond flour, tahini, and vinegar in a bowl. Stir in remaining ingredients. Mash together all ingredients and shape into patties with wet hands. Bake on baking sheet 25 minutes, flipping once. Serve with roasted red pepper sauce *(in condiments section of cookbook)*.

Cold Chicken Whole Wheat Pearl Couscous Salad

Ingredients
1 cup chicken, cooked, diced, cooled
1 cup whole wheat couscous, cooked, cooled
½ cup leeks, diced
½ cup zucchinis, diced
1 cup cherry tomatoes, halved
1 can black beans, drained
¼ cup rice bran oil
2 Tbsp seasoning *(I use Mrs. Dash Fiesta® brand)*
2 Tbsp apple cider vinegar

Directions
Combine chicken, couscous, and vegetables. Mix seasoning, vinegar, and rice bran oil in small bowl. Pour over chicken mixture. Let chill 15 minutes.

Spicy Spinach Salad with Toasted Pumpkin Seeds

Salad ingredients
2 large eggs, beaten lightly
4 cups baby spinach
1 cup bean sprouts
1 cup shredded carrots
½ cup shredded red cabbage
½ cup toasted, unsalted pumpkin seeds
2 green onions, diced

Dressing ingredients
1 Tbsp lime juice
1 Tbsp rice bran oil
½ tsp chile sauce *(I use Sriracha® brand)*
¼ cup ginger, grated

Directions
Coat skillet and cook egg like an omelet. Cool on cutting board. Cut into strips. Stack 5 or 6 spinach leaves and cut into long slivers. Repeat until spinach is gone. Top with carrots, cabbage, sprouts, onions, pumpkin seeds, and eggs. Pour dressing on top.

BWC (Brussels Sprouts, Walnuts, Cranberries)

Ingredients
½ cup walnuts, chopped
2 tsp rice bran oil
½ cup shallots, diced
1½ lbs Brussels sprouts, halved
1 tsp garlic, minced
½ cup dried cranberries
1 Tbsp agave nectar
1 tsp walnut oil

Directions
Heat a large skillet. Add and warm walnuts 4 minutes and set aside. Wipe skillet. Add rice bran oil, making sure entire pan is coated. Add Brussels sprouts, cooking 5 minutes. Add shallots and garlic, cooking 1 minute. Stir in cranberries, agave nectar, and 1 cup of water. Partially cover skillet with lid and reduce heat to medium, simmering 5-7 minutes, or until sprouts are tender *(not soft)*. Transfer to serving dish and top with walnut oil and toasted walnuts.

Roasted Veggies

Ingredients
2 red peppers, cleaned and cut into 8" strips
1 green pepper, cleaned and cut into 8" strips
2 zucchinis, cut into thick strips
1 yellow squash, cut into thick strips
1 red onion, cut into wedges
1 bunch asparagus
1 bunch broccoli
2 tsp seasoning *(I use Bragg® brand)*
2 sprays liquid aminos *(I use Bragg® brand)*

Directions
Preheat oven 450°F. Spray a cookie sheet with cooking spray and arrange veggies. Drizzle with olive oil and 2 sprays of liquid aminos. Add seasoning. Cook 25 minutes.

Note: Liquid aminos are similar to soy sauce, only healthier!

Green Goddess Dip

Ingredients
10 oz frozen spinach
14 oz can artichokes, quartered
4-6 oz mascarpone *(Italian cream cheese)*
4 garlic cloves
¼ cup cheese, chopped
5 green onions, sliced thin
Pinch salt
Few dashes hot sauce
Mini sweet bell peppers *(for dipping)*

Directions
Preheat oven 350°F. Process spinach, mascarpone, garlic, and hot sauce. Mix artichokes, green onion, and chopped cheese. Place mixture in baking dish of choice. Bake in oven until bubbling and golden brown, roughly 30 minutes. Serve with crackers or raw vegetables of choice.

Kookie Monster Dip

Ingredients
½ cup sun butter
2 cup almond flour
¼ cup honey
¼ cup agave nectar
1 Tbsp vanilla extract
½ cup walnuts or cashews, finely chopped
½ cup chocolate chips *(I use Enjoy Life® brand)*
½ cup chocolate candies *(I use SunSpire™ brand)*

Directions
Combine all but last three ingredients. Mix well. Add remaining ingredients. Refrigerate 15 minutes.

Ideas for dippers: pretzels, apples, graham crackers, animal crackers

Spicy Sweet Potato Dip

Ingredients
1 lb sweet potatoes, peeled and cut into 1" pieces
1 can chick peas, drained and rinsed
$\frac{1}{8}$ cup fresh lemon juice *(from 1 lemon)*
3 Tbsp chili sauce *(I use Sriracha® brand)*
$\frac{1}{4}$ cup tahini
2 Tbsp coconut oil, melted
2 tsp ground cumin
1 garlic clove, minced
2 green onions *(for garnish)*

Directions
Bring pot of water to a boil and add sweet potatoes. Cook until tender, roughly 10 minutes. Transfer to food processor. Add remaining ingredients to sweet potatoes, except green onions. Puree until smooth *(you may need to add a tsp of water from the sweet potatoes to make it thinner)*. Season with salt and pepper, adding green onions on top. Refrigerate in a glass dish. It will keep for about a week.

Chocolate Quinoa Protein Granola Bars

Ingredients
¾ cup dry quinoa
½ cup dates, pitted
3 Tbsp agave nectar
2 Tbsp rice bran oil
2 Tbsp ground flax seed
½ tsp almond extract
¼ tsp salt
½ cup your favorite protein powder
½ cup coconut flour
½ cup your favorite stir-ins *(Enjoy Life® mini chocolate chips, shredded coconut, or dried fruit will work)*

Directions
Preheat oven 350°F and spray an 8x8" pan. Rinse dry quinoa in cold water and let sit in a bowl of water for 10 minutes. In the meantime, bring 1 cup of water to boil. Drain quinoa and add to boiling water. Cover, and reduce heat to simmer about 12 minutes. Let cool. In the bowl of a food processor, combine cooked quinoa, dates, agave nectar, vegetable oil, flaxseed, almond extract, and salt. Process until relatively smooth. In a small bowl, stir together protein powder, flour, and stir-ins. Fold this dry mixture into wet mixture with a spatula. *The dough is very thick, like cookie dough, so use the spatula to press into prepared pan evenly.* Bake 22-25 minutes, until firm. Let cool. Slice into one dozen bars. Store in an airtight container for up to a week, or freeze up to 3 months.

primitive plates

Turkey Taco Wraps

Ingredients
1 Tbsp rice bran oil
1 tsp garlic, minced
1-2 Tbsp green chiles, diced
1 tsp ground cumin
¼ tsp cayenne
1½ lbs ground turkey
½ tsp salt
½ cup green onions, thinly sliced
1 large bunch cilantro, finely chopped *(about 1¼ cups chopped cilantro. I used 1 cup in tacos and ¼ cup in salsa. Use more or less cilantro to taste.)*
2 Tbsp fresh lime juice
2 large heads romaine lettuce *(or use iceberg, Boston, or butter lettuce)*

Directions
Heat rice bran oil in heavy frying pan. Add minced garlic and diced green chiles, and sauté about 1 minute. Add cumin and cayenne and cook about 1 minute. Add turkey, salt, and cook over medium-high heat, breaking apart with back of a utensil. Cook 5 minutes, or until turkey is starting to brown.

While turkey cooks, thinly slice green onions and set aside. Wash cilantro, spin dry or dry with paper towels, and finely chop cilantro. Cut off root end of lettuce, discard tough outer leaves, wash, and spin dry in a salad spinner or dry with paper towels.

When turkey is lightly browned, add green onions and cook 2 minutes. Remove from heat. Stir in 1 cup chopped cilantro and 2 Tbsp lime juice.

Homemade Toppings for the Taco Wraps
2 medium avocados, diced
1½ cups cherry tomatoes, finely chopped
¼ cup cilantro, finely chopped
2 Tbsp fresh lime juice
2 Tbsp olive oil *(optional)*

Directions
Place avocados in glass or plastic bowl and toss with lime juice. Stir in tomato, cilantro, and olive oil. Spoon 2-3 large spoonfuls of turkey mixture into each piece of lettuce. *(I used the inner, more folded pieces of lettuce and saved the flatter outer pieces for using in salad).* Top meat mixture with salsa *(you could put this mixture into a wheat tortilla).*

Fresh Grilled Tuna Salad

Ingredients
2 lbs fresh tuna steak, 1" thick
2 tbs olive oil *(for brushing tuna)*
2 ½ tsp sea salt
½ tsp fresh ground black pepper
2 lime zest, grated
1 tsp wasabi powder *(optional)*
6 Tbsp lemon juice, squeezed
2 tsp low sodium soy sauce
2 tsp hot sauce
2 ripe avocados, diced
¼ cup leeks, chopped
½ cup cherry tomatoes, diced
½ cup cucumbers, chopped
4 slices bacon, cooked and crumbled

Directions
Brush tuna steak with olive oil and sprinkle with sea salt, pepper. Place tuna steaks in a very hot pan or on grill. Cook 1 minute on each side. Let rest on a platter. In a small bowl, combine remaining olive oil, pepper, lime juice, lime zest, hot sauce and wasabi powder. Mix well. In a medium bowl, combine cherry tomatoes, cucumbers, leeks, and bacon. Add liquid mixture to it. Cut tuna steak. Pour mixture over tuna.

Other suggestions: add spinach, kale, cooked whole-wheat couscous

Buffalo Stuffed Acorn Squash

Ingredients

1 bunch kale, clean and chopped
2 acorn squash, halved lengthwise and seeded
6 cloves garlic, chopped
1 leek, chopped
1 lb ground buffalo
1 pint baby bellas, chopped
2 small zucchini, quartered and chopped *(about 2 cups)*
2 peppers, any color, chopped
1 cup of cherry tomatoes, halved
1/3 cup of dried cherries, roughly chopped
1 Tbsp dried thyme
1 Tbsp ground cumin
A pinch of nutmeg

Directions

Preheat oven 400°F. Place acorn squash in a baking dish, skin side up. Drizzle with a little extra virgin olive oil, or give it a light spray with non-stick olive oil spray. Add about an inch of water to the bottom of the pan, and pop in the oven 30 minutes. *You want the squash to be tender, but not completely cooked, because it will be going back in for another 10-15 minutes after you stuff it.*

While squash is cooking, heat a Tbsp of extra virgin olive oil in a large sauté pan. Add leeks and kale. Cook 3 minutes before stirring in garlic and a pinch of salt. Allow garlic, leeks, and kale to cook another 3-5 minutes. Push leeks, kale, and garlic aside and add ground buffalo, breaking it up. Add peppers, mushrooms, and zucchinis to the pan, along with thyme, cumin, nutmeg, a little more salt, and pepper. Bring everything together as it is cooking. Once veggies are cooked, add tomatoes and dried cherries. Let everything heat 15 minutes.

Turkey Pesto Meatballs

Ingredients
½ cup panko bread crumbs
2 cloves garlic
½ cup packed basil
2 Tbsp pine nuts
¼ cup parmesan cheese
1 large egg
½ tsp salt
¼ tsp pepper
1¼ lbs ground turkey

Directions
Preheat oven 375°F. Add garlic, basil, pine nuts, parmesan, egg, panko bread crumbs, salt and pepper to food processor. Cover and pulse until well combined. Transfer mixture to mixing bowl. Add ground turkey. Combine well and form into balls. Line baking sheet with aluminum foil and spray with cooking oil spray. Cook 25-30 minutes, flipping once.

Fiesta Boats

Ingredients
4 zucchini
1½ Tbsp olive oil
1 cup leeks or onions, chopped
2 cloves garlic
3 Tbsp jalapeno, chopped
1½ tsp chili powder
½ tsp cumin
1 lb lean ground turkey
1 tomato, chopped
½ cup fresh corn
½ cup fresh guacamole
¼ cup grated sharp cheddar cheese *(optional)*

Directions
Preheat oven 375°F. Clean out cores of zucchinis, *(do not break)*. On a cutting board, dice up insides of zucchinis along with leeks, and transfer to a pan with olive oil. When garlic is tender, add cumin, jalapenos, and turkey. Cook mixture 7 minutes, breaking turkey as you go. When turkey is cooked, remove from pan. Put in dish with tomatoes and corn. Fill zucchini boats with this filling *(ok to overflow)*. You can top with cheese if you would like. Cook 25-30 minutes.

Mini Turkey Meatloaves

Ingredients
2 lbs turkey
½ cup fresh parsley
½ tsp cayenne pepper
½ tsp coriander
1 Tbsp olive oil
¼ cup almond flour
1 cup zucchini, finely chopped
½ cup onion, finely chopped

Directions
Preheat oven 400°F. Grease a cupcake tin with coconut oil. Form mixture into 12 balls and put into cupcake pan. Bake 20-30 minutes.

Chicken Marsala

Ingredients
4 5 oz boneless, skinless chicken breasts
½ tsp salt
½ tsp dried thyme
⅛ tsp ground black pepper
2 tsp olive oil
16 oz mushrooms, sliced
1 large shallot, finely chopped
2 garlic cloves, minced
½ cup dry Marsala wine
½ cup reduced-sodium chicken broth

Directions
Pound chicken breasts to ½" thickness and sprinkle with salt, ¼ tsp of dried thyme, and pepper. Heat 1 tsp of olive oil in a large, nonstick skillet over medium-high heat. Working in batches if necessary, add chicken *(without overcrowding the pan)* and cook until browned/cooked, about 4 minutes on each side. Remove from pan and place on a plate lined with a paper towel. Heat remaining 1 tsp of oil in skillet. Add mushrooms, remaining salt, and thyme. Cook, stirring occasionally, until mushrooms are slightly browned, roughly 5 minutes. Add shallots and cook, stirring often, until shallots start to soften, about 2 minutes. Add garlic and stir for about 1 minute. Add Marsala and broth. Cook until sauce thickens slightly, about 1 minute. Return chicken back to skillet and cook until heated through, about 2 minutes.

Apple, Jalapeno Stuffed Chicken

Ingredients
4 large chicken breasts
2 jalapeno peppers, diced
1 McIntosh apple, peeled and cored
¼ cup Parmesan cheese
4 oz chicken sausage, cooked and crumbled
1 Tbsp Cajun seasoning
½ tsp cumin

Directions
Preheat oven 350°F. Slice a slit in each chicken breast to accommodate stuffing. In a large mixing bowl, combine apples, jalapeno peppers, Parmesan cheese, chicken sausage, and seasonings. Mix well. Place stuffing inside pouches of the chicken, and place on a lightly-oiled baking pan lined with aluminum foil. Use toothpicks, if needed, to hold chicken together. Cook 25-30 minutes, or until chicken is cooked.

Pulled Miss Piggy (Pulled Pork)

Ingredients
4-5 lbs pork butt
2 yellow onions

For The Rub
2 Tbsp chili powder
1 tsp dried parsley
2 tsp cumin
2 tsp onion powder
¼ tsp chipotle powder
2 tsp sea salt

Directions
Mix all dry ingredients together and rub over roast. Layer bottom of slow cooker with half of onions. Add roast and remaining onions on top. No water necessary. Cook 5-6 hours on high. Turn to low for another 2 hours.

Bok Choy Skillet

Ingredients
2 tsp rice bran oil
8 oz button mushrooms, sliced
10 cherry tomatoes, halved
½ cup leeks, finely chopped
1 cup bulgar
1 cup mushroom broth
1 tsp fresh thyme
4 small bok choy, halved

Directions
Heat oil in a skillet, then add mushrooms and leeks. When cooked, set aside. In the same pan, add tomatoes. Cook 1 minute and place with mushrooms and leeks. Add 1 tsp of oil to the skillet and brown bulgar until golden. Add broth to bulgar, reduce heat, and cover. Simmer 5 minutes. Arrange bok choy on top of bulgar. Add mushroom mixture and tomatoes around skillet. Simmer 5 minutes. Top dish with fresh thyme.

Cubanella Stuffed Peppers

Ingredients
6 Cubanella peppers, cleaned and halved
1 cup couscous, cooked
1 cup buffalo or turkey *(ground)*, cooked
½ cup yellow and red peppers, diced
¼ cup fresh corn
¼ cup fresh salsa
2 tsp seasoning *(I use Mrs. Dash Fiesta® brand)*

Directions
Preheat oven 350°F. In a skillet, cook your ground buffalo or turkey. Add in corn, diced peppers, and seasonings, mixing well. In a separate pot, cook couscous until al dente. Add to the mixture in the skillet, along with the salsa. Cut the peppers in half and remove the seeds. On a cookie sheet, place peppers and fill to top with mixture. Cook 1 hour.

Pumpkin, Apple, Bacon Soup

Ingredients
1 medium pumpkin, seeded and chopped
1 Tbsp olive oil
8 pieces turkey bacon
1 large leek, chopped
6 stalks celery, chopped
6 carrots, chopped
1 bay leaf
2 tsp curry powder
1 tsp dried thyme
1 Granny Smith apple, peeled, cored, and cubed
4 cloves garlic, minced
½ cup apple juice
1½ liters unsalted chicken stock

Directions
Preheat oven 190°F. Drizzle pumpkin with olive oil. Roast 30-40 minutes. Cook bacon, leaving drippings in pan. Add leek, celery, carrots, bay leaf, curry, thyme, salt, and pepper to pan. Cook until tender. Add apples and cooked pumpkin. Cook 5 minutes. Stir in garlic and cook 1 minute. Pour in apple juice. Reduce heat and simmer until liquid is reduced by half. Stir in chicken stock and simmer over medium-low heat 45 minutes. Puree and serve with bacon or yogurt on top.

PBAB Sandwich

Ingredients
1 lb ground buffalo
4 large Portobello mushrooms, cleaned
8 pieces turkey bacon
1 avocado
4 romaine lettuce leaves
1 tsp olive oil

Directions
Form buffalo into patties. Brush mushrooms with olive oil. Place buffalo burgers and mushrooms on grill. Cook bacon separately in pan. Slice avocado. Stack all ingredients on top of mushroom.

Buffalo Chili

Ingredients
2 lbs ground buffalo
1 bell pepper, cleaned and diced
6 cloves garlic
2 tsp olive oil
3 Tbsp cumin
4 Tbsp chili powder
1 tsp dry oregano
1 can tomatoes
1 cup water

Directions
In a deep casserole dish, add garlic and oil. Add peppers and buffalo and cook 5 minutes. Add tomatoes, mashing and mixing throughout. Add water and seasoning. Reduce heat to low and let simmer for 2 hours.

Cold Asian Noodles with Pork Loin

Ingredients
2 medium carrots, halved lengthwise and thinly sliced crosswise
2 English cucumbers, halved lengthwise and thinly sliced crosswise
½ jalapeno pepper, seeded and thinly sliced
½ cup unseasoned rice vinegar
1 Tbsp fish sauce
4 oz rice vermicelli noodles
1½ lb pork tenderloin
3 Tbsp rice bran oil
1 Tbsp hoisin sauce
2 cups romaine lettuce, thinly sliced
1½ cups fresh cilantro or basil

Directions
Put carrots, cucumbers, and jalapenos in a bowl. Heat rice vinegar and fish sauce in saucepan and pour over veggies. Add salt and pepper to taste. Stir to mix the sauce on the vegetables. Heat water to a boil and add vermicelli noodles. Remove from heat and let stand 8 minutes. Drain with cold water. Season pork with salt and pepper. Heat a Tbsp of rice bran oil in a skillet, adding pork and cooking roughly 3-5 minutes each side. Brush loin with hoisin sauce. Turn again and cook 1 minute. Remove meat from skillet to a cutting board and let rest 5 minutes. Slice thinly. Divide noodles among bowls. Strain pickled vegetables, reserving the liquid. Stir hoisin sauce and remaining rice bran oil into reserved liquid. Drizzle over noodles and top with pork and pickled vegetables, lettuce, and herbs.

Pesto Chicken Stuffed Avocado

Ingredients
1 cup chicken breast, shredded
2 Tbsp pesto *(recipe found in sauce section of cookbook)*
3 Tbsp low fat natural yogurt
4 avocados, halved and seeded

Directions
Combine all ingredients together. Gently fill avocados with chicken mixture. Serve immediately.

PankoCoco Fish Sticks

Ingredients
1 cup almond flour
½ cup coconut flakes
½ cup panko crumbs *(plain)*
2 tsp sea salt
2 tsp garlic powder
½ tsp lemon pepper *(I use Mrs. Dash® brand)*
½ cup olive oil
3 lbs white fish, cut into 1" pieces

Directions
Preheat oven 350°F. Combine flour, coconut flakes, and spice in food processor. Pulse into meal. Place mixture into small bowl. In another bowl, place panko crumbs. Pour oil in a small bowl. Start by dipping into oil, followed by almond mixture, and panko crumbs. Bake 20 minutes, or until lightly browned.

Lemon Dill Salmon

Ingredients
4 salmon fillets
*(frozen is ok,
but thaw first)*
Juice of 1 lemon
1 tsp lemon zest
2 tsp walnut oil
1 tsp dill
2 cloves garlic, minced

Directions
Preheat oven 450°F. Put all ingredients, except sea salt, into a Ziploc® bag. Marinate 20 minutes. Take salmon out and place on an ungreased baking dish, skin side down. Cook 14-17 minutes, or until cooked. *(I used an ungreased baking dish so the salmon skin sticks to the pan.)*

Spaghetti Squash with Meat Sauce

Ingredients

2 Tbsp coconut oil, divided
1 leek, chopped
1 ½ lbs ground buffalo
1 cup water
1 ½ cans *(9 oz)* tomato paste
2 Tbsp red wine vinegar
2 cloves garlic, minced
1 tsp salt
Freshly ground black pepper, to taste
1 tsp Italian seasoning
1 pinch cinnamon
1 large spaghetti squash *(about 3 lbs)*
¼ tsp freshly ground black pepper
12 cherry tomatoes, red or yellow *(or a combination of both)*, halved
½ cup fresh Parmesan or Pecorino Romano cheese shavings
2 Tbsp fresh flat-leaf Italian parsley, chopped

Directions

Prepare meat sauce. In a large saucepan, heat 1 Tbsp of coconut oil over medium heat. Add leeks and sauté until translucent, about 5 minutes. Transfer leeks to a plate, leaving oil in pan. Brown meat in reserved oil over medium-high heat, stirring to break into even crumbles. Return leeks to pan. Add water, tomato paste, vinegar, garlic, cinnamon, and Italian seasonings. Let sit 2 minutes.

Preheat oven 350°F. Line a baking sheet with parchment paper. Cut squash in half, lengthwise, and scoop out seeds. Place squash, cut-side-down, on prepared pan. Bake until flesh can be easily scraped into strands with a fork, roughly 50-70 minutes. Remove from oven and let cool slightly. Using a fork, scoop out flesh into a bowl and fluff spaghetti-like strands. Toss in salt and pepper. Place on a large, warmed platter, or cleaned squash shell.

Melt remaining coconut oil in a small saucepan over medium heat and cook until light brown. Pour over squash strands. Toss with a fork to blend. Top squash with hot meat sauce. Scatter tomatoes over squash and meat sauce and sprinkle with cheese and parsley.
Serve immediately.

Chicken BLTA Sandwich

Ingredients
1 chicken breast
(¼-⅓ of top cut off)
2 slices bacon, cooked
1 handful arugula
or spinach
1 tomato, halved
and thinly sliced
1 avocado, peeled
and smashed

Directions
Butterfly chicken breast *(cut lengthwise so it can be opened up like a book)*. Heat a little oil in a pan and cook chicken, opened up, 4-6 minutes, or until browned. Flip chicken over and cook, covered, for an additional 5-10 minutes *(depending on thickness)*. Remove from pan and spread avocado inside. Add remaining ingredients.

Paleo Pizza Crust

Ingredients
2 cups almond flour
1 cup arrowroot powder
1 ½ tsp baking powder
1 ½ tsp salt
1 ½ tsp oregano
¼ tsp black pepper
3 eggs
½ cup almond milk

Directions
Preheat oven 425°F. Grease a round pizza pan or cookie sheet. Combine dry ingredients in a large bowl. Whisk to blend together, adding eggs and almond milk to dry ingredients. Mix well *(the batter will be runny, not like typical pizza dough).* Use a spatula to spread batter onto greased pan. Bake crust in preheated oven 8-12 minutes. Remove crust from oven and top with sauce and desired toppings. Bake 10-15 minutes.

Optional add-ins: Cooked chicken, buffalo, sausage, veggies of any kind, fresh herbs.

Tacos Shells Paleo Style

Ingredients
2 cups almond flour
2 large eggs
1 tsp oil
½ tsp salt taco toppings choice *(ground buffalo seasoned with taco seasoning in this cookbook, lettuce, tomatoes, taco sauce or salsa, avocado, olives, onions, etc.)*

Directions
Preheat oven 350°F. Combine flour, eggs, oil, and salt in a bowl and mix until well blended. Roll out balls of dough between two pieces of parchment paper to desired thickness *(⅛" thick or so)*. Remove top layer of parchment paper and place bottom layer with dough onto a baking sheet *(I put 3 tortillas on a sheet at a time)*. Bake 6-10 minutes or until desired "crispness" is achieved.

Lemon Chicken Bake

Ingredients
2 ½ Tbsp lemon juice
½ tsp pepper
¾ tsp salt
3-4 garlic cloves, pressed
¼ cup rice bran oil
4 chicken breasts
1 onion
2-3 carrots
1 large sweet potato
½ cup zucchini and red peppers

Directions
Preheat oven 375°F. Combine lemon juice, pepper, salt, garlic, and oil or butter in a bowl. Cut up onion, carrots, sweet potato, red peppers, and zucchini into wedges or chunks. Baste chicken with a bit of lemon mixture. Pour remaining lemon mixture over veggies and stir to coat. Place chicken and veggies in a large pan and bake 45-60 minutes, or until chicken is cooked and veggies are tender.

Veggie Stir Fry

Ingredients
1 bunch kale
2 leeks, cleaned and diced
2 green zucchinis, diced
1 red pepper, cored and diced small
1 yellow pepper, cored and diced small
1 bunch asparagus, trimmed and cut into bite-sized pieces
2 Tbsp coconut oil
2 Tbsp seasoning *(I use Bragg® brand)*

Directions
In a large skillet, add coconut oil, peppers, asparagus, leeks, and zucchinis, and cook for 2 minutes. Turn off heat and add kale.

Beef and Barley Soup

Ingredients

2 ½ lbs beef short ribs
1 *(14 oz can)* diced tomatoes with juice
1 cup pearl barley
1 large yellow onion, diced small
2 large carrots, peeled & finely chopped
5 stalks celery
1 sprig fresh thyme
½ cup Italian/flat leaf parsley
1 bay leaf
4 cups beef broth *(low sodium)*
1 handful dried wild mushrooms, rehydrated in hot water for 10 minutes, drained and chopped. Add liquid to soup.
1 Tbsp rice bran oil
Salt and freshly ground pepper to taste

Directions

In a large soup pot or Dutch oven, combine ribs, tomatoes, barley, onion, carrots, fennel, thyme, and bay leaf. Add liquid. Heat at medium-high and bring to a boil *(there will be foam that rises to the surface; skim it off)*. Lower heat to simmer and cover for 2 hours, stirring occasionally. Remove bay leaf and thyme/parsley sprigs. Heat oil in a skillet over medium-high heat. Add sliced mushrooms and sauté until mushrooms are golden. Add to soup and continue to simmer 1 hour, or until meat falls off bones. Remove bones, shred/dice meat, and return to soup.

Grilled Flank Steak Asian Style

Ingredients
2 lbs buffalo flank steak or beef flank steak
1 Tbsp rice bran oil
Salt and freshly ground black pepper
2 cloves garlic, chopped
2 Tbsp ginger, peeled and chopped
1 stalk green onion, chopped
2 Tbsp liquid aminos
(I use Bragg® brand)
½ tsp dark sesame oil

Directions
Score steak on one side in crisscross pattern. Rub steak with oil, and season both sides with salt and pepper. In a small bowl, combine remaining ingredients. Rub mixture all over scored side of steak. Marinate 24 hours and grill to your liking.

desserts

Peppermint Patties

Ingredients
1 banana
1 can coconut milk's thick coconut cream *(extra liquid poured off and not mixed in)*
4 Tbsp coconut oil, melted
2 tsp peppermint extract *(or to taste)*
1 Tbsp honey
1 cup semisweet chocolate chips *(the darker the better)*
2 Tbsp coconut oil
Sheet parchment or wax paper
10 wax-lined small Dixie® cups

Directions
In blender, combine banana, coconut cream, melted coconut oil, and peppermint extract. Pour about ¼" deep into wax-lined small Dixie® cups, and freeze at least 2 hours. Once patty centers are frozen, melt coconut oil and chocolate chips in microwave and stir. Working quickly, remove patties from freezer and peel cup away. Dip frozen patties in melted chocolate and lay out on parchment paper to cool. Store in fridge or freezer. Serve cool.

Almond Butter Bites (My version of Reese's Peanut Butter Cups®)

Ingredients
1 cup semi-sweet chocolate chips *(I use Enjoy Life® brand)*
½ cup almond butter

Directions
On very low heat, melt chocolate in a pan or double boiler. With a clean utensil, paint chocolate in any candy mold and put directly into freezer for 10 minutes. Fill hardened chocolate with almond butter. Paint remaining chocolate over almond butter and place back into freezer for 10 minutes. *Be careful when trying to take out of candy molds.*

Pumpkin Cookies

Ingredients
½ cup organic pumpkin puree
2 Tbsp honey
2 eggs
4 Tbsp coconut flour
¼ tsp baking soda
¼ tsp sea salt
1 tsp cinnamon
1 Tbsp butter or coconut oil, room temperature
½ cup chocolate chips *(I used Enjoy Life® brand)*

Directions
Preheat oven 400°F. Cover a baking sheet with parchment paper. Combine eggs, pumpkin puree, and honey. Mix all dry ingredients in a separate bowl and add to pumpkin mix. Add chocolate chips and mix thoroughly. Drop Tbsp-sized balls of dough onto cookie sheet and bake 10-12 minutes. Let cool on a cookie rack 10 minutes.

Other options: nuts (any kind), apples instead of pumpkin, bananas

Snowballs

Ingredients
1 cup walnuts, unsalted
1 cup almonds, unsalted
1 cup dried dates, pits removed
½ cup mini chocolate chips *(I use Enjoy Life® brand)*
¼ cup raw honey
¼ cup almond flour
¼ cup coconut oil, melted
½ cup coconut flakes

Directions
Place walnuts and almonds in a food processor. Blend. Set aside in a medium bowl. Add dates to food processor and puree until almost a paste. Add honey and coconut oil to date mixture. Mix well. Add flour mixture to nut mixture. Add date mixture to dry mixture, stirring well. Add mini chips. Form into balls and roll in coconut flakes. Refrigerate.

Mango Lime Sorbet

Ingredients
4 cups frozen mango
½ cup agave nectar
¼ cup fresh
lime juice

Directions
Partially thaw mangos. Place in blender and puree with agave nectar and lime juice. Place in dishes or freeze pops. Freeze 30 minutes.

Lemon Dream Bars

Ingredients
6 eggs
½ cup honey
½ cup coconut oil
1 cup lemon juice
½ cup unsweetened coconut flakes

Crust
1 cup almonds
1 cup macadamia nuts
¼ cup honey
½ cup coconut oil, melted
2 eggs

Directions
In a small sauce pan, whisk eggs, honey, and lemon juice together on medium heat. Add coconut oil. Stir until coconut oil melts and mixture starts to thicken. Once thickened, remove from heat, put in a bowl, and store in refrigerator to cool.

Preheat oven 400°F. Place almonds and macadamia nuts in a food processor and blend until in small chunks. In a small bowl, combine nuts with honey, eggs, and melted coconut oil. Mix well. Grease an 8x12" baking pan and spread nut mixture on bottom. Bake 15-18 minutes. Cool *(it is important to make sure it cools completely)*. Spread lemon mixture over crust and sprinkle top with coconut flakes. Return to refrigerator.

Chocolate Chip Cookies

Ingredients
¾ cup coconut flour
½ tsp sea salt
½ tsp baking soda
1 tsp cinnamon
½ cup coconut oil, melted
4 eggs
6 dates
3 Tbsp coconut milk
1 Tbsp vanilla extract
½ cup unsweetened shredded coconut
1 bag chocolate chips *(I use Enjoy Life® brand)*

Directions
Preheat oven 350°F. Line a baking sheet with parchment paper. Put dates into a food processor until evenly consistent *(you may need to add lukewarm water)*. In a small bowl, whisk together all dry ingredients. In a large bowl, mix together eggs, melted coconut oil, vanilla, coconut milk, and date mixture. Slowly add dry ingredients into the wet and mix with a spoon until smooth. Add chocolate chips and coconut to mixture. Spoon cookie mixture onto baking sheet and bake 10-12 minutes. Transfer to cooling rack.

Watermelon Ice Pops

Ingredients
1 mini watermelon, cut up and rind removed
1 can coconut milk
¼ cup honey

Directions
Put all ingredients into a blender and mix well. Spoon mixture into ice pop molds. Freeze 1 hour.

Dark Chocolate Almond Butter Cups

Ingredients
½ cup almond butter
⅛ tsp salt
1 Tbsp arrowroot
1 tsp vanilla
1 cup dark chocolate chips, divided

Directions
Melt ½ cup dark chocolate chips in a double boiler. Line a mini muffin pan with 16-18 mini-muffin papers. With a basting brush, brush bottoms halfway up sides of mini muffin papers. Refrigerate. In a bowl, mix together almond butter, salt, arrowroot, and vanilla. Take mini muffin pan out of refrigerator and divide almond butter mixture evenly among cups. Melt remaining ½ cup of chocolate chips in double boiler. Spoon chocolate on top of almond butter mixture and spread to cover completely. Return to refrigerator until chocolate hardens. Store in refrigerator.

Note: The very first batch I made into 12 cups - they were rich! The second batch I made into 16 cups and the third batch I made into 20 cups. It depends on how much chocolate and almond butter you want per cup. I prefer the 20 chocolate cups.

Oatmeal Cream Cookies

Ingredients
1 cup creamy almond butter
1/3 cup raw honey
2 tsp vanilla extract
3 Tbsp water
1 Tbsp chia seeds, ground
(I ground mine in a coffee grinder)
1 1/2 - 2 tsp cinnamon
1/8 tsp nutmeg
Scant less than 1/2 tsp salt
1/2 tsp baking soda
1/2 cup unsweetened, shredded coconut
1/2 cup raisins

Directions
Preheat oven 350°F. Mix all cookie ingredients together in a large bowl. Allow to set a few minutes so the chia will bind the batter. Line a cookie sheet with parchment paper. Drop spoonfuls of dough onto paper. *(I made mine small so I could make a lot of oatmeal cream pies. You can also make them big and have giant ones.)* Bake cookies 8-12 minutes, or until lightly browned on top. Remove cookies from oven and press down gently with a small piece of parchment paper to flatten *(be careful not to push too hard, breaking the cookies)*. Cool completely.

Marshmallow Cream Ingredients:
1 cup water, split in half
1 cup raw honey
1 Tbsp gelatin *(1 packet of gelatin is slightly less than 1 Tbsp)*
1 tsp vanilla extract
Pinch of salt

Marshmallow Cream Directions:
Put 1/2 cup water and gelatin in a large bowl. Set aside. Put the other 1/2 cup water, honey, vanilla, and salt in a medium saucepan and cook over medium heat. When mixture begins to boil, insert a candy thermometer. Continue to boil until mixture reaches 240°F *(which is soft-ball stage)*. Remove mixture from stove and slowly pour into bowl with gelatin. Mix on high with wire whisk attachment on a stand mixer. Mix until thick like marshmallow cream, up to 10 minutes. Spread cream on bottom-side of a cookie, as thick as you'd like. Top it off with another cookie to make a "sandwich."

No-Bake Cookies

Ingredients
⅓ cup honey *(reduce amount of honey to your liking)*
1½ Tbsp cocoa
⅓ cup coconut oil or butter
⅓ cup almond butter
1 tsp vanilla
2 cups unsweetened, dried coconut

Directions
Put honey, cocoa, and coconut oil in a medium saucepan over medium-high heat. Bring mixture to a boil. Boil 1 minute and immediately remove from heat. Stir in almond butter and vanilla until incorporated. Stir in coconut. Scoop by spoonfuls onto wax or parchment paper and put in refrigerator until hardened and set.

Banana Bread

Ingredients
½ cup mini chocolate chips *(optional. I use Enjoy Life® brand)*
1½ cups mashed bananas *(about 2½ bananas)*
5 eggs
¼ cup applesauce
¼ cup coconut oil, melted
¾ cup honey
1½ tsp vanilla
1 cup arrowroot
¾ cup coconut flour
1 tsp baking soda
½ tsp salt

Directions
Preheat oven 300°F. Grease 9×5" bread pan. Put mashed bananas, eggs, applesauce, butter or oil, honey, and vanilla in a large bowl and mix well. Add dry ingredients and chocolate chips. Mix well. Pour batter into prepared bread pan and bake at 300°F 1 hour and 20-25 minutes, or until knife inserted comes out clean.

condiments

Lemon Dressing

Ingredients
2 medium lemons
3 Tbsp shallots, finely chopped
3 Tbsp spicy mustard
½ tsp Kosher salt
½ tsp agave nectar
¼ cup olive oil

Directions
Squeeze lemons, making sure to not get any seeds in the bowl. Add shallots, mustard, salt, agave nectar, and olive oil. Mix well. Use immediately, or store in refrigerator for up to 1 hour.

Roasted Red Pepper Sauce

Ingredients
1½ cup roasted red peppers, drained
½ cup toasted almonds
1 clove garlic
2 tsp red wine vinegar

Directions
Puree all ingredients in food processor.

Kale Pecan Pesto

Ingredients
12 oz bunch of kale, stems removed, leaves torn
¼ cup toasted pecan pieces
2 cloves garlic, peeled
⅓ cup olive oil
½ cup parmesan cheese, grated
½ cup water

Directions
Place kale in a large pot with water. Cook 5 minutes, or until kale is wilted, but still bright green. Drain and save water. Set aside to cool. Blend pecan pieces with garlic in food processor until finely chopped. Add cooked kale and blend until thick paste forms. Add oil and 2 Tbsp of cooled kale water. Blend until smooth.

Mustard Barbeque Sauce

Ingredients
1 cup yellow mustard
2 tsp Worcestershire sauce
¼ cup red wine vinegar
¼ cup white vinegar
1 tsp light brown sugar
Freshly ground black pepper

Directions
Whisk mustard, Worcestershire sauce, red wine vinegar, white vinegar, brown sugar, and pepper into a bowl. Refrigerate until ready to serve.

Basic Vinaigrette

Ingredients
⅓ cup sugar
1 small onion, finely diced
¼ cup apple cider vinegar
¼ cup unsweetened apple sauce
2 Tbsp water
2 Tbsp rice bran oil
4 tsp mustard
1 tsp sea salt
½ tsp fresh ground black pepper

Directions
Combine all ingredients in blender or food processor. Mix well. Transfer into glass container and refrigerate.

Homemade Apple Butter

Ingredients
1 quart apple sauce
2 Granny Smith apples, peeled, cored, and cut into chunks
2 Tbsp brown sugar *(I used Sucante® brand)*
1 tsp cinnamon

Directions
Stir ingredients into slow cooker. Cook on low 3 hours, with lid off, stirring occasionally. Store apple butter in refrigerator. *If jars are sealed properly, you can store apple butter in the pantry until you're ready to serve.*

Homemade Taco Seasoning

Ingredients
½ cup chili powder
¼ cup onion powder
⅛ cup ground cumin
1 Tbsp garlic powder
1 Tbsp paprika
1 Tbsp sea salt

Put all ingredients into a mason jar and shake well.

Note: 3 Tbsp of the Homemade Taco Seasoning is equal in sodium to one 4 oz store-bought package of taco seasoning.

Homemade Spaghetti Sauce

Ingredients
2 roma tomatoes, cored
1 red bell pepper, cored
⅓ cup red wine vinegar
⅓ cup sun dried tomatoes, coarsely chopped
6-8 basil leaves
Juice of 1 lemon
Dash sea salt
1 cup water

Directions
Blend all ingredients and half of water until smooth. Add more water until desired consistency. Refrigerate unused portions. Makes about 3 cups.

Creamy Avocado Dressing

Ingredients
2 avocados, peeled and pitted
Juice of 1 lemon
Juice of 1 lime
1 tsp lime zest
1 cucumber
½ cup water
¼ cup cilantro, chopped
½ - 1 tsp chili powder
Dash sea salt

Directions
Blend all ingredients together until smooth, adjusting water to get desired consistency. Refrigerate unused portions. Makes 3+ cups.

Basic Stocks

Ingredients
4-5 lbs of chicken, turkey parts, or meaty bones
1 large onion, chopped
2-3 large carrots, chopped
3-4 stalks celery *(the leafy top parts are great for stock as well)*
6-8 garlic cloves, chopped
1 Tbsp whole black peppercorns

Directions
Put all ingredients into a pot and simmer 2 hours. Periodically skim off foam as it rises to top of pot. When finished cooking, strain broth and refrigerate 2 hours. Any fat in broth will congeal at the top and can be easily strained off. Stock is now ready for use or for the freezer.

Vegetable Stock

Ingredients
2 cups large yellow onions, diced
2 cups large leeks *(green and white parts)*, diced
2 cups mushroom trimmings, wiped clean
1 cup large carrots, diced
1 cup large celery, diced
1 cup large turnips, diced
1 cup large parsnips, diced
1 cup large yellow squash, diced
1 cup large zucchini, diced
8 cherry tomatoes, quartered
½ cup garlic cloves, peeled
2 Tbsp rice bran oil
1 Tsp salt
½ tsp fresh cracked black pepper
1 gallon water
2 Tbsp fresh thyme, or 2 tsp dried
8 parsley stems
4 basil stems
2 whole bay leaves
2 cups white wine

Directions
Preheat oven 400°F. In a large roasting pan, spread onions, leeks, mushrooms, carrots, celery, turnips, parsnips, squash, zucchini, tomatoes, and garlic. Drizzle with rice bran oil and season with salt and pepper, stirring to coat. Roast 45 minutes, stirring every 15 minutes to brown evenly. Remove from oven and transfer to a large pot. Add water and herbs and bring to a boil. Reduce heat and simmer 20 minutes, skimming to remove any foam that rises to the surface. Add wine and cook 30 minutes. Remove from heat and strain through a fine mesh strainer into a clean container. Use immediately or cool in an ice bath and refrigerate in an airtight container for up to 5 days. The stock can be frozen up to 3 months.

Beef Stock

Ingredients
7 lbs beef bones, sawed into 2" pieces
1 6 oz can tomato paste
2 cups onions, chopped
1 cup celery, chopped
1 cup carrots, chopped
2 cups Claret wine
20 peppercorns
5 garlic cloves, peeled
5 bay leaves
1 tsp dried leaf thyme
1 ½ gallons water

Directions
Preheat oven 400°F. Place bones on a roasting pan and roast 1 hour. Remove from oven and brush with tomato paste. Lay vegetables over bones. Return to oven and roast 30 minutes. Place pan on stove and deglaze with wine, scraping bottom of pan for browned particles. Put mixture in a large stock pot. Add peppercorns, garlic, and herbs. Season with salt. Bring liquid to a boil and reduce to a simmer. Cook 4 hours. Remove from heat and skim off any fat that has risen to surface. Strain liquid and discard bones.

CrossFit TUFF
New School Knowledge, Old School Attitude

145 A Temple Street Nashua NH 03060
603-557-5556

Yesterday I dared to struggle, Today I dare to win...

"It starts with a dream.

Add faith,
and it becomes a belief.

Add action,
and it becomes a part of life.

Add perseverance,
and it becomes a goal in sight.

Add patience and time,
and it ends with a dream come true."

- Doe Zantamata

❖ ❖ ❖

"The food you eat can be either
the safest & most powerful
form of medicine or the
slowest form of poison."

- Ann Wigmore

❖ ❖ ❖

"There is no diet that will do
what eating healthy does.
Skip the diet, just eat healthy."

Made in the USA
Lexington, KY
04 September 2013